Harriet Pilpel
"The commission that reported in 1970 did not call for the suppression of sexually related materials as detrimental to our society...Indeed the commission report urged more sex education, more information, more openness about sexuality..."

Max Lillienstein
"Well-reviewed sex education books intended for teenage audiences are often stocked in a back room or under the counter after a visit from a police officer, citizens group, or minister."

Ann Welbourne-Moglia
"I speak for the victims who have not been heard from...but will be chained for life to sexual ignorance."

Arlene Carmen
"Freedom...and ...conscience will have no place in a society where government espouses a particular religious view of morality, one that has no room for deviation from the norm."

Donald Mosher
"No consensus exists among scientists about any alleged dangerous effects of pornography."

Anthony Schulte
"...Publishers are extremely concerned with... legislating against the freedom of expression that is essential, not only for literature and reading, but for the very essence of the American pluralistic society."

Lisa Duggan
"...problems...are best addressed by increasing women's power to control our lives...what we are being offered instead is a return to the pedestal where vice squads and prosecutors can 'protect' us from dirty pictures and tell us what to read and see."

Richard Green
"...In the United States there is no relation between the sale of pornography and the rape rate."

Betty Friedan
"My own book, The Feminine Mystique,...was suppressed as pornographic."

Eve Paul
"The federal Comstock laws...passed in 1873... prohibited mailing..."obscene" or "immoral" matter. Until 1971 this...included medicine for the prevention of contraception..."

Lisa Duggan
"Obscenity laws...have nev

Communications

Donald Mosher	"...Your right to sexual privacy includes your right to choose to include or exclude pornography... Preserve that freedom of choice or everyone becomes less free."
Betty Friedan	"I urge all women to have their eyes opened to the dangers to our basic rights by the pushing of antipornography legislation."
Donald Mosher	"Sex offenders read the Bible and <u>Newsweek</u> too without it causing either inherently good or evil mental states and actions."
Lisa Duggan	"This commission is a cynical manipulation of women's hopes for a better life. Let's stop sexism, not sex."
Betty Friedan	"Underneath the sideshow, they are trying to excite passions of people against ideas... not actual deeds, not violence...to take our attention away ...while we are being manipulated, and our rights are being threatened...The obscenity that threatens us...taking away school lunch, milk supplements and medical benefits away from old people and reducing social security."
Arlene Carmen	"We are being asked to...believe that domestic violence and rape will be eliminated by the suppression of nude photographs."
	"The road to thought and behavior control is short, narrow and dangerous."
Barry Lynn	"The evidence they are gathering is both skewed and superficial."
	"In their zeal to keep sexual content away from children they seem on the verge of reducing the adult population of America to seeing only what is fit for a seven year old."
Max Lillienstein	"The commission has refused the American Booksellers Association an opportunity to testify."
Harriet Pilpel	"Our fundamental freedoms...rest not on the will of the majority but on the protection of minorities and individuals who disagree with the majority."

M E E S E   C O M M I S S I O N   E X P O S E D

Proceedings of an NCAC Public Information Briefing

on

The Attorney General's Commission on Pornography

January 16, 1986

New York City

NATIONAL COALITION AGAINST CENSORSHIP
132 West 43rd Street
New York, N.Y. 10036
(212) 944-9899

INTRODUCTION

A week before the New York Hearings of the Meese Commission on Pornography, the National Coalition Against Censorship held a Public Information Briefing to protest and publicize the bias of the Commission and its likely outcome.

Author Kurt Vonnegut, actress Colleen Dewhurst, and feminist Betty Friedan were among the 14 speakers, from Planned Parenthood, the American Booksellers Association, the Feminist Anti-Censorship Taskforce and other prominent organizations. Their full remarks are printed here.

Representatives of all major media attended the briefing along with 150 representatives of literary, artistic, religious and social groups important in American life.

"We are deeply concerned at the direction the commission is taking," said NCAC Executive Director Leanne Katz. "Censorship, with all its dangers, seems inevitable."

Katz and other speakers categorized the Meese Commission's five prior hearings as a "kangaroo court." The majority of the witnesses were police vice officials, obscenity prosecutors, so-called pro-decency groups and anonymous "victims" who testified from behind screens about abuse allegedly caused by sexually-explicit materials. The commission took no initiative in inviting writers and artists, or others who might help them assess the impact of censorship on creativity and communication. Few witnesses explored the implications of censorship.

"Although there is no consensus about the effects of

sexually related expression, the commission seems ready to impose restrictions based on its beliefs," said Ms. Katz. "Serious and long-lasting impact on our system of free expression is inevitable."

NCAC PUBLIC INFORMATION BRIEFING ON THE MEESE COMMISSION ON PORNOGRAPHY

THURSDAY, JANUARY 16, 1986, AT 10:45 AM, CAFE 43, 147 W 43 ST NEW YORK CITY

I'm Leanne Katz, executive director of the National Coalition Against Censorship, and I welcome you to our public information briefing on the Attorney General's Commission on Pornography.

NCAC is a broad-based coalition of 41 national nonprofit organizations, including some of the largest and most important groups in American life. We are joined to defend the idea that all of us have a right to read and write and listen and speak and think for ourselves.

Twelve years ago a series of Supreme Court decisions restricted, more than previously, First Amendment protection for so-called obscene expression. There was widespread concern at these restrictive decisions, and as a result NCAC was born. Today we are seeing on the local, state, and federal levels a seriously growing wave of attacks on sexually related expression. Right now in North Carolina, for instance, a new obscenity law has led to police targeting R-rated and PG-rated videos; a chain of video stores has removed <u>Victor Victoria</u>, <u>Passage to India</u>, and <u>Splash</u>, among many other movies, from fear of arrest; and a First Amendment scholar who teaches at the University of North Carolina has changed his teaching about obscenity law lest he face criminal prosecution. I am told that the FBI there has stopped people coming out of video stores to ask them what they have rented or bought.

Next Tuesday, the Meese Commission on Pornography,

headed by Henry Hudson, a Virginia prosecutor who has just been elevated to the post of U.S. Attorney for Northern Virginia, will hold the last of its hearings scheduled for six cities around the country. Part of its charge is to make recommendations about pornography not only to the Department of Justice for proposed new federal legislation, but to local and state governments.

In a press release announcing the commission, Attorney General Meese is quoted as saying that its formation is related to "the achievement of the good life and the good society." Some of us who follow today's Justice Department are a little dubious about its ability to help us with that undertaking.

Here and there in the hearings, there are sprinklings of rationality. But the overall tone is set by a parade of what the commission calls "victims," by prosecutors who specialize in pornography, and by police from vice and morals squads. The "victims" testify anonymously from behind screens to sad personal experience -- allegedly caused, pure and simple, by pornography. The cops testify as specialists in child molestation and the harmful effects of pornography.

All in all, it's a tawdry picture. The setting is not inspiring for a national debate on such momentous questions as whether or how this country should censor sexually explicit expression -- or, in the words attributed to Mr. Meese: how to achieve the good life and the good society.

It is remarkable to examine the list of the commission's

2

topics for what it reveals about what it has failed to consider. Restrictions on sexually related expression invariably affect literature and the arts, communication and entertainment, education and intellectual inquiry -- just for starters.

So it is a real scandal is that the commission has made no attempt on its own to invite testimony from, for example, one single writer -- not a fiction writer, a journalist, or a reporter -- nor so far as I am aware, a single artistic group, or any writers' organization in this entire country. Moreover, when the organizations themselves initiated requests to the commission, they met with resistance, stalling, and obstruction.

This briefing is to impart some sense of the broad range of views which are being ignored while important social policy is under consideration. The remarks of the people we invited should make us all stop and think -- and worry -- **and** then act, to fight censorship.

HARRIET PILPEL

In 1970, another distinguished commission reported on the subject of obscenity and pornography. Although the word pornography is commonly used as if it had a clear definition, it has no specific meaning in our law. Something that is "pornographic" therefore cannot be made illegal unless it's obscene in addition -- if it is obscene the word pornography is superfluous.

The commission that reported in 1970 did not call for the suppression of sexually related materials as detrimental to our society. Indeed, that commission report urged more sex education, more information, and more openness about sexuality instead of any kind of repression. These recommendations were reached after extensive research, investigation, and a broad-based look at the behavior of men and women in many walks of life.

The present commission has not yet issued its report. At a business session in Miami, however, they came up with a working definition of pornography which apparently satisfied them, namely, "A representation is pornographic if it is designed to be sexually arousing and portrays children, pain, humiliation and sexual abuse, conduct or organs as a dominant theme." This definition is so vague it could be impossible to apply. Such a definition could chill all kinds of speech and do much harm. The commission has commissioned no new research; a woman called Judith Reissman was given $750,000 by the U.S. Department of Justice to investigate the illustrations in three popular so-called pornographic magazines. Her budget for this dubious research was criticized by many people -- especially since it was larger than the amount allotted to the commission for all its work.

Some of us may be personally offended by the deluge of sexually explicit materials now available in the marketplace. Of course, we need not rent or buy home videos of sexually related movies or look at the explicitly detailed magazines or listen to music with erotic lyrics. The times have changed in some ways from twenty years ago. The coming of cable television and home videos has increased the number of options from which people can choose what things they want to see and hear. And it turns out that many of them want to see sexually-related matter which appears to have a large audience.

However, the principle of free expression does not change. It's easy to embrace freedom of speech for ideas we accept. The essence of freedom of speech and the press is that we must protect the ideas we hate. Many efforts have been made to show that there is a connection between so-called pornographic materials and illegal sex behavior. As of the present time, there is no scientific evidence to support such a conclusion. At times it looks as if scientific research and careful study have been brushed aside in favor of unsubstantiated testimony from anonymous witnesses. It seems to me and many others, that more sexual information, not less, will serve our society better.

Positive attitudes toward sexually related materials can help our children more than labelling it as taboo and forcing it into underground channels.

Although those in favor of suppressing so-called pornography assume it leads to criminal activities, this has not been proved. I don't think it ever will since I don't think it's so.

A victim with a sad tale of child abuse may say that his father read explicitly sexually arousing magazines, but so do thousands of other fathers who do not engage in child abuse. The facts involved are always far more complex than one single element. In the hundreds of years before sexually explicit magazines and videos were available, there was rape and child abuse, cruelty and murder.

Proponents of any kind of prohibitions on speech and the press are in a very fundamental sense anti-American. For our fundamental freedoms -- such as our freedom of speech and the press rest not on the will of the majority but on the protection of the minorities and individuals who disagree with the majority. Our basic belief is: Though I disagree with every word you say, I will fight to the death for your right to say it.

Actors' Equity was dismayed to see that the people who had been testifying at the Meese Commission did not include theater organizations, playwrights, actors, writers, everybody who affected our profession, which is probably the true victim of the onslaught that we see now because we deal in free speech, in the extension of ideas, in terms of expressing the human condition as it is and as the writer sees it and as the citizen of the United States sees it.

Actors' Equity began to approach the commission over and over again to ask that one of us, as a representative, be allowed to testify. We received no answer. And we continued. Finally, we received an answer, saying yes, we could testify -- but on the final day in New York, at 6:45 I believe. And our darling, good, Equity said that's not a good time for an actor to speak, at 6:45, God forbid you should have a job. Plus the fact that she'll have no audience. So as of last week the commission said that we could speak at 1:45. I am particularly interested because we are representing a membership that would be one of the most threatened by having their work suddenly termed obscene or not obscene. The artist knows better than anyone that one man's obscenity is another man's delight.

When <u>Mrs. Warren's Profession</u> was written in 1896 by George Bernard Shaw, it was shown only in private theaters in England. It was not shown in what we would call a commercial theater. It opened here in 1905 at the Garrett Theatre, and was closed that night and the actors were arrested. I just want to read one short excerpt from Mrs. Warren's Profession.

This is Mrs. Warren, talking to her daughter:

"Where can a woman get the money to save in any other business? Could you save either four shillings a week and keep yourself dressed as well? Not you. Of course if you're a plain woman and can't earn anything more, or if you have a taste for music or the stage, or newspaper writing, that's different. But neither Liz nor I had any turn for such things. All we had was appearance and our turn for pleasing men. Do you think we were such fools as to let other people trade in on our good looks by employing us as shop-girls or barmaids or waitresses when we could trade in ourselves and get all the profits instead of starvation wages? Not likely. What is any respectable girl brought up to do and do for a living? Catch some rich man's fancy and get the benefit of his money by marrying him. As if a marriage ceremony could make any difference in the right or wrong of the thing -- oh, the hypocrisy of the world makes me sick."

Thirty years after it first came here it was finally produced on Broadway again.

When they did Strange Interlude in 1928 and they entered Boston, they were told that they could not play there because in the third act, abortion was mentioned and getting rid of the fetus. So they went to Quincy and they bused them there. They thought it was a Cardinal who had gone after them and they looked into it and found out that it was not. It was a boss -- a very high-placed boss, who wanted a $10,000 lawyer's fee to defend them.

When Moon for the Misbegotten opened in Detroit, the headline that Armina Marshall saw when she opened the paper next morning was "Moon for the Misbegotten closed for obscenity." So they went to the police. Marshall asked what had happened. This policeman said that they mentioned "mother" and "prostitute" in the same sentence. That was an obscenity, and they were closing the show.

She said, "You just had Maid of the Ozarks here and you're going to close Moon for the Misbegotten written by a Pulitzer Prize winner?"

He said, "I don't care what he wins. I won't have any dirty plays here in Detroit."

She said, "What about Maid of the Ozarks?"

He said, "Maid of the Ozarks ran because I helped them rewrite it."

She said, "I don't think Mr. O'Neil would care to have you rewrite this play."

So finally James Dunn, who played the lead, came in and said, "All right, we'll take out eight words."

By then it had become such a farce that the newspapers were there, and the cop turned around and said, "Please take a picture of me with these two ladies."

And Armina Marshall said, "Over my dead body."

That's the danger and the question -- who determines who

closes us. And for what reason.

The government should not have the power to rule art.

I have read much of the heart-rending testimony extracted from victims of sexual abuse at meetings of the Attorney General's Commission on Pornography. It is clear to me that our Government must be given the power to suppress the words and images which are the causes of sexually motivated insanity and crimes. As the Bible says: "In the beginning was the word."

I myself make my living with words, and I am now ashamed. In view of the terrible damage freely circulated ideas can do to a society, and particularly to innocent children, I beg my government to delete from my works all thoughts which might be dangerous. I want the help of our elected leaders in bringing my thoughts into harmony with their own and thus into harmony with the thoughts of those who elected them. That is democracy.

Attempting to make amends at this late date, I call to the attention of the Attorney General's Commission on Pornography, and God bless the attorney general, the fundamental piece of obscenity from which all others spring, the taproot of the deadly poisonous tree. Kill the taproot and the tree dies, and with it its deadly fruits, which are rape, sodomy, wife-beating, child abuse, divorce, abortion, adultery, gonorrhea, herpes, and AIDS.

I will read this most vile of all pieces of so-called literature aloud, so that those who dare can feel the full

11

force of it. I recommend that all persons under 14, and all persons under 30 not accompanied by an adult, should leave the room. Those remaining who have heart trouble or respiratory difficulties, or who are prone to commit rape at the slightest provocation, may want to stick their fingers in their ears. And what I ask you to endure so briefly now is what the selfless members of the pornography commission do day after day for the good of our children. I am simply going to dip you in filth, and pull you out of it and wash you off immediately. At terrible risk of infection, they have to wallow in pornography. They are so fearless. We might think of them as sort of sewer astronauts.

All right. Everybody ready? Tighten your G-strings. Here we go:

"Congress shall make no law respecting an establishment of religion, or prohibiting the free exercise thereof; or abridging the freedom of speech, or of the press, or the right of the people peaceably to assemble, and to petition the Government for a redress of grievances."

That Godless loop of disgusting sexuality, friends and neighbors, happens to be a basic law of this country. How could this have happened? Some communistic, pederastic, wife-beating congressman, while we weren't watching, must have tacked it onto the Rivers and Harbors Bill. It should be expunged with all possible haste, in order that innocent children can be safe again.

Adolph Hitler blamed the Jews for inspiring every sort

of sexual ugliness in Germany, so he tried to kill them all.
Say what you like about him, incidentally, it can't be denied
that he led an exceedingly clean life sexually. In the end,
he made an honest woman of his only sexual partner, Eva
Braun.

Oh dear -- have I slipped into pornography yet again?
It is so easy to do.

Hitler was wrong about the Jews. It is unclean images
which are responsible for unclean sexuality.

In order to protect innocent German children, all he had
to do was get rid of the First Amendment. In no way can this
be interpreted as an anti-Semitic act. The authors of that
amendment, Thomas Jefferson and James Madison, were not Jews.

It is not enough that sex crimes of every sort are
already against the law, and are punished with admirable
severity. It is up to our leaders, and particularly to our
attorney general, to persuade a large part of our citizenry
that even the most awful sex crimes are perfectly legal, and
even celebrated in some godless quarters, because of the
permissiveness of our Constitution. Only then will an
aroused and thoroughly misinformed citizenry rise up in
righteous wrath to smash the First Amendment -- and many
other only slightly less offensive parts of the Bill of
Rights.

Once the findings of the Attorney General's Commission
on Pornography are published for all to see, whether they can
read or not, what sort of American would dare to defend

13

liberty, whose cost is so horrible? I'll tell you what kind

of an American, friends and neighbors: the sort of American

who would rape a three-year-old girl, drench her in lighter

fluid, set her ablaze, and throw her off a fire escape.

As we used to say in geometry class back in public

school when I was a boy: "Q.E.D. -- quod erat demonstrandum."

I thank you for your attention.

BARRY LYNN

The Attorney General's Commission on Pornography has a problem understanding three little subjects. Unfortunately, these topics are American culture, the Constitution, and sex. Their hearing in Washington, where I testified, as well as the gatherings in Chicago, Los Angeles, Houston, and Miami where I have travelled to watch them, are genuinely frightening to people who worry about government censorship. This morning I would like to highlight briefly just a few of the deficiencies of their approach.

First, the evidence they are gathering is both skewed and superficial. They have viewed an endless display of graphic slide shows, as if locating the single most grotesque portrayal of sexual behavior ever photographed will somehow justify the most intrusive and Draconian new efforts to suppress all sexually explicit material. They have also adopted a "victim impact" approach to pornography, in which a stream of mostly anonymous witnesses, concealed behind screens, tell very sad life stories of abuse -- all supposedly linked to pornography. No matter how outrageous the claims, the commissioners ask no probing questions to assess their veracity, or the actual role of pornography in these witnesses' troubled lives. They didn't even bother to question one witness's claim that her life was jeopardized just by appearing. Moreover, whenever it is apparent that pornography is only tangentially connected to the witnesses' very real problems of child abuse, drug dependence, or divorce, the commissioners themselves lead them back toward emphasis on the "porn-link." With this lack of serious cross-examination, no witness is ever discredited, and unchallenged assertions provide legitimacy to the commissioners' legion of antipornography biases. Treatment of anticensorship witnesses is quite different. The chairman of the commission, Henry Hudson, a zealous antipornography prosecutor from Virginia, for example, constantly pressed my colleague and me on whether the ACLU had ever received funds from the Playboy Foundation (we have), as if a few coins would corrupt the policies of an organization that predates Playboy by thirty years. Although they claim an interest in hearing even from those who do not wish to curtail sexually explicit material, there is no real incentive for such persons to come forward. The few voices they have heard in that direction are dismissed as irrelevant because they are deemed either doctrinaire -- like the ACLU -- or financially self-interested.

Second, since the charter of this commission includes the charge to find new ways to "control the spread of pornography," they eagerly listen to, and then adopt, virtually every extreme law enforcement initiative suggested by any antipornography witness -- everything from statutorily defining the depiction of certain sexual activites as obscene per se to utilizing racketeering statutes against publishers. They have been convinced that pornography is invading the home through new technologies like "dial-a-porn," cable

16

television, and rock music. In their zeal to keep sexual content away from children they seem on the verge of reducing the adult population of America to seeing only what is fit for a seven year old.

Third, in 1970, a previous pornography commission suggested that all legal restraints on adult access to sexually-oriented material were unconstitutional and should be repealed. This body hasn't even seriously considered such a position. They gave tentative approval to major changes in law enforcement a month before they concluded that any harms even flowed from the existence of pornography. When one commission member pointed out the peculiarity of operating in this order, the staff director said that if the commission didn't find harms, they could just "throw the whole thing out." Perhaps one reason that constitutional issues are rarely even whispered about is that the only constitutional "expert" on the commission is a law professor who has written that pornography has no First Amendment protections at all because reading pornography is just like visiting a prostitute or using a dildo.

Last May, when this commission was announced, I indicated to the press that I feared a train marked "censorship" had left the Washington station. It has now gotten to about Colorado and hasn't left the track.

ANNE WELBOURNE-MOGLIA

I was invited to speak at the Commission on pornography
hearings held in Houston in September. I was very pleased
that the commission wanted information about the relationship
between sex education and pornography, and the implications
legislation might have on education and training.

When I arrived in Houston the Straight Slate was holding
a press conference in the park across from the courthouse.
The Straight Slate supports a heterosexual government. In
front of the courthouse, picketers carried plaques to outlaw
filth. In the courtroom itself, the pewlike benches were
filled predominantly by priests with tape recorders and women
with notepads. The press box was essentially empty. TV
cameras appeared twice: when the "victims" of pornography
testified, and when the commissioners toured a local adult
bookstore in the evening.

I spoke on the second day of the hearings, after lunch,
to an audience of approximately 15 people. I believe my
testimony was well received by the commissioners. There is
not enough time now to summarize the information and key
points of my testimony. Copies are available.

In the time given me today, I want to speak for the
victims who have not been heard from, who will not hold press
conferences or picket, and who will not be asked to speak
before the commission, but will be chained for life to sexual
ignorance. These victims are:

The children who are growing up not understanding their

bodies and feeling guilty and confused about sexuality.

The millions of adolescents who are pregnant, becoming parents, getting abortions, dropping out of school, taking drugs, facing a future with limited horizons, and considering suicide. Why? Because they do not know and have not been helped to understand and handle their sexuality.

The millions of parents who feel overwhelmed and afraid and unprepared to teach and talk with their children about sexuality.

Half the couples in the United States who have not learned how to communicate about their sexual desires and concerns.

The disabled and disenfranchised who have been told sexuality is a privilege and not to be a part of their lives.

And finally, the majority of Americans who learn most of what they know about sexuality from each other, in an atmosphere of secrecy and confusion.

Our President, our Attorney General, and, I fear, the commission on Pornography, want to legislate sexuality and censor information about it. They see pornography as a "clear and present danger." Speaking as an advocate for victims, myself one of them, I would like to say that the real clear and present danger is ignorance. We must do everything we can to stop this sexual ignorance epidemic. We must not censor information. We must provide our citizens with the information and skills they need to make their own responsible decisions about their sexuality.

19

DONALD MOSHER

At the Houston hearings of the Attorney General's Commission on Pornography, I testified that scientific knowledge was based on a social consensus of scientists formed around properly gathered and interpreted empirical evidence. No consensus exists among scientists about any alleged dangerous effects of pornography.

The Reagan administration has gutted behavioral and social scientific research by withholding research funds. Yet, Edwin Meese would like to justify the containment of pornography by finding scientific evidence of its harmful effects. His approach is to spend no money to do the necessary research, bring together political constituencies to testify at six hearings, lump in some social scientists with their own crosses to bear, and create a Tower of Babel in which witnesses speak in passionate, confused, biting, and forked tongues. Out of the scientific uncertainty and conflicting testimony, strands of information can be selected to form a crazy patchwork quilt of supposed evidence pointing to alleged harms. When science is misused to support a preconceived ideology, skeptical limitations vanish and gaps in knowledge are bridged by "facts." A closed mind looks less empty when it quotes scientists. An ideologue disguised in sheep's clothing is still a wolf at the door of civil liberties.

No sooner had I finished testifying in Houston and entered the courtroom lobby, when I ran into another lobby.

I had indicated in my testimony that no scientist, given the structure of the hearings, could possibly meet the criteria of an adequate scientific review of the effects of pornography. David A. Scott lobbied me, a mere scientist and not a legislator. He gave me his purported review of the effects of pornography on the family, community, and culture, which he claimed met scientific criteria. His tract on pornography was published by the Free Congress Research and Educational Foundation. No scientific journal would publish such misinformation -- an alloy of scant evidence and Religious Right ideological bias. According to reporter William Ryan, Jerry Falwell sponsors this group.

In 1868, Lord Cockburn formulated a flawed but influential test of obscenity: "I think the test of obscenity is this, whether the tendency of the matter charged as obscenity is to deprave and corrupt those whose minds are open to such immoral influences and into whose hands a publication of this sort may fall." Adherents to such legal moralism and legal paternalism still believe they "know pornography when they see it." They, moreover, need to protect other adults -- who without harm to others, voluntarily seek to experience sexual arousal from it -- because pornography causes inherently evil mental states. If, as the wag would have it, pornography is the literature read with one hand, I presume such "containment" would keep both hands, as well as the mind, empty.

Scott, writing for the Free Congress Foundation, takes

the antipornography program further than usual when he argues
that the bottom line effect of normal people being exposed to
sexual materials, including prime-time TV and sex education,
is a "malignantly-regressive 'primitivization' of emotional
relatonships" -- mental health jargon misappropriated to
describe inherently evil mental states and actions.
Organized crime, the media, sex educators, and the schools --
an orgy of strange bedfellows -- market deviance as not
deviant, according to Scott's gospel. Scott's argument is a
version of domino theory applied to evil mental states: First
normal people are desensitized and then corrupted by
pornography. Second, not content just to devalue monogamy,
normal people's appetite for more bizarre pornography and
sexual fantasy to incorporate into sexual activity increases.
Third, an addiction to even more deviant pornography forms.
Fourth, now addicted, rapists and other dangerous offenders
require soft-core porn to produce the fantasies required to
support the act of rape. Fifth, the "fix" (porno-sex)
becomes as urgent and frequent as an addict's need for
chemical substances, producing massive numbers of sex
offenses.

Humans love to pose little remedies for big troubles. A
little remedy, like containment of pornography (particularly
when packaged with such symbols as God, Country, and Family),
for such big troubles as dangerous threats to family
(endangered monogamous marriage), community (dangerous sex
crimes), and culture (the marketing of deviance as not

deviant) can seem appealing. Too bad it is a quack remedy.

Furthermore, First Amendment rights guaranteeing both separation of church and state and freedom of expression are threatened. How can the Free Congress Foundation be treated as a nonprofit educational organizaton by the IRS? How long will acceptance of a doctrine like "lust in your hearts" lead to an equation of sexual fantasy with sexual sin or deviance. Pornography is a form of collective sexual fantasy. Freedom of expression underlies freedom of thought. Containment of pornography threatens freedom of expression and inquiry. As a scientist of sex, if pornography is contained, can I study its effects? And if pornography is so pernicious because it produces "malignantly-regressive" (evil?) sexual arousal and fantasy, when does the campaign begin to control people's sexual fantasies? Is masturbation far behind? Why not, to preserve the family, all nonprocreative sex within marriage or without? Book burning is the weapon of choice in Mind Control.

Censors make the arrogant, paternalistic, moralistic assumption that others (but never them) are harmed or corrupted by pornography. Fred Berger, the philosopher, recently posed three necessary conditions for censorship and argued that none of them are met by pornography. First, there must be strong evidence of a _very_ likely and serious harm. There is no such strong scientific evidence; hence, little consensus.

Second, the harms must be closely and directly linked

with the expression. Pornography has not been so linked to serious harms. Pornography is neither hate propaganda against women nor the addictive progenitor of sex crimes. Unfortunately, some pornography is sexist; more unfortunately, it is no more sexist than prime-time TV. Feminists against pornography have entered into a curious alliance with the Right in posing a litle remedy, containment of pornography, for such a serious trouble, societal sexism. The "I know a sex offender who read pornography" claim is not scientific evidence of causal connection; sex offenders read the Bible and Newsweek too without it causing either inherently good or evil mental states and actions.

Third, Berger argues, it must be unlikely that further speech or expression can be used to effectively combat the harm. The scientific evidence, although weak, is just as strong that debriefing following exposure to pornography in the laboratory can reverse the attitudes that were initially changed through exposure.

The 1970 report of the President's Commission on Obscenity and Pornography was unfairly maligned, and its recommendations were never implemented. Yet, its plea for further scientific research and massive sex education remains the best guide to public policy.

Since children cannot give informed consent to sex -- they neither understand the implications nor are they powerful enough to choose freely when solicited by adults -- the only pornography requiring containment is child

pornography exploiting children. Philosopher Joel Fineberg
had argued that pornography is not so much a menace as a
nuisance and that nuisance laws provide adequate legal
protection against unwanted exposure. As consenting adults,
your right to sexual privacy includes your right to choose to
include or exclude pornography from your sexual life.
Preserve that freedom of choice or everyone becomes less
free.

These hearings, supposedly "fair," "balanced," and
"open" attempts to gather information and evidence about the
effects of pornography, are in fact a biased, manipulative
charade. The Feminist Anti-Censorship Taskforce (FACT) is
protesting the hearings and the commission as a danger to
women's right to free expression.

The commission, appointed by Attorney General Ed Meese,
was created by the Reagan Administration, which has
distinguished itself for its hostility to the rights of
women. Cutbacks in programs designed to serve women and
children, and the erosion of affirmative action, are now
being joined by this attack on women's right to sexual
expression.

Commission Chair Henry Hudson, a zealous vice prosecutor
from Virginia who shut down every adult bookstore in his
jurisdiction, pretends the commission is open-minded and
fair, interested in finding and hearing the truth about
sexually explicit materials. But truth is beside the point.
The commission has been charged with finding "more effective
ways in which the spread of pornography could be contained."
Its membership is stacked with moral conservatives, and
witness lists have been slanted to give a platform to vice
cops, the FBI, and anti-porn crusaders. The commission staff
claims to be making a serious effort to find qualified
witnesses, but many experts with contrary points of view have
been turned away. The commission is dead-set on assembling

phony "facts" and "testimony" that will support the draconian new censorship measures that the Reagan Administration has in mind and that the staff has already drafted. So far, the commission has considered:

Beefing up existing obcenity laws by adding heavy fines and mandatory jail sentences.

Increasing government surveillance of private individuals suspected of trafficking in pornography.

Recommending new legislation including measures to regulate cable TV, computer communication and phone lines.

Drafting model statutes such as one designed to curtail the sale of "rubber goods" used in sexual stimulation, including vibrators.

As feminists, we are especially appalled that this latest attempt to restrict freedom is being disguised as an effort to "protect" women. We believe that the problems women have with sexism in pornography are best addressed by increasing women's power to control our lives. We also need resources and services to help us regain control when we are abused, and redress against those who discriminate against us or threaten us. What we are being offered instead is a return to the pedestal where vice squads and prosecutors can "protect" us from dirty pictures, and tell us what to read and see.

Obscenity laws and other methods of increasing state control over private life and sexual expression have never benefited women. Historically, obscenity laws like the

Comstock Act have been used to restrict information about birth control and abortion, to limit public sex education, and to seize literature and art. It is not hard to guess the targets of new, more severe obscenity laws -- feminist and gay bookstores, art galleries, video shops, sex education including AIDS health information materials, and the new erotica that women themselves are now producing.

This commission was appointed to appease the demands of the religious right for a society-wide effort to "clean up filth," and to overturn the 1970 President's Commission Report on Obscenity, which found no reason for state regulation of sexually explicit material. This new report is scheduled to appear in June, 1986, just in time to whip up public hysteria for the fall election campaigns. The commission will spend $500,000 of your tax dollars to manipulate public fear and discomfort with sexuality in order to foment a modern morality crusade. Politicians will be pressured to respond with new censorship legislation.

A coalition of feminist groups, Feminists Against the Meese Commission (FEMCOM), protested at the Los Angeles hearings in October. FACT has had observers present at all commission hearings, and we testified before the commission in Chicago this past July. At that time we made clear our desire to see something meaningful done to improve the lives of women and to enhance both our freedom and our safety. But this commission is a cynical manipulation of women's hopes for a better life. Let's stop sexism, not sex.

The scientific data show that the _more_ pornography is available, the _fewer_ the sex crimes committed.

In Denmark in 1967, pornography, including child pornography, could be bought by anyone over age 15. During the next six years, the rate of child sexual assault dropped 67 percent.

In West Germany, pornography was legalized in 1973. During the next eight years, sex offenses against children under age six dropped 60 percent. Thus, the experience in these nations contradicts the thesis that more pornography is associated with an increase of sex crimes against women and children.

The explanation for the finding is that pornography provides an outlet for antisocial sexual impulses. It permits the person to experience, safely, in fantasy, what would otherwise have been acted out, violently, with a victim.

In Great Britain, along with the increased availability of pornography, rape rates did not rise as much as nonsexual assaults. In fact the British Committee on Obscenity and Film Censorship concluded that there was "(no) support at all to the argument that pornography acts as a stimulus to the commission of sexual violence."

In Japan, the most common form of pornography depicts rape, yet the Japanese rape rate is one-sixteenth that of the United States. In the United States as a whole, concurrent with the great increase in pornography between 1970 and 1978, the rape rate did not rise disproportionately to the rate of nonsexual assault.

Regionally, in the United States, there is no relation between the sale of pornography and the rape rate. However, other factors are related. They include alcohol consumption, poverty, and the circulation of another type of magazine -- the outdoor magazine -- such as <u>Field and Stream</u> and <u>Guns and Ammo</u>.

In 1900, the practice of contraception in the United States was condemned by the law, public opinion, and organized medicine. The federal Comstock laws, named after their principal advocate, Anthony Comstock, were originally passed by Congress in 1873. These laws -- vestiges of which remained in force until 1983 -- prohibited mailing, shipping, or importing "obscene" or "immoral" matter. Until 1971, this was defined to include articles, drugs, or medicine for the prevention of conception and the dissemination of certain printed materials about contraceptives. The Comstock laws also prohibited the mailing of "every article or thing designed, adapted, or intended for producing abortion" or material giving information as to where or how abortion could be obtained.

Anthony Comstock, the secretary of the New York Society for the Suppression of Vice, boasted that he had destroyed more than fifty tons of indecent books, 28,425 pounds of plates for the printing of such books, almost four million obscene pictures, and 16,900 negatives for such pictures. There is reason to believe that Attorney General Meese's Commission on Pornography is in the Comstock tradition of censorship.

On October 16, 1916, Margaret Sanger, a nurse who had seen at first hand the tragedies in women's lives that resulted from the unavailability of birth control, opened the first center for contraceptive instruction in the United

States. Sanger and her sister showed people how to use cervical caps, condoms, and other contraceptives. The police closed the clinic and arrested Margaret Sanger and her sister for violation of a New York statute that prohibited the giving of information about birth control. After serving 30 days in prison, Sanger in 1921 founded the American Birth Control League, which is today the Planned Parenthood Federation of America.

Since then, public opinion about contraception and abortion has changed a great deal. The American public today supports the availability to women and men of a full range of fertility control services. Moreover, public opinion supports sexuality education as well as the provision of contraceptive services to teenagers in the public schools.

Since 1942, the federal government has supported the provision of family planning services to those who cannot afford them, most significantly under the Family Planning Services and Population Research Act (Title X of the Public Health Service Act), which was enacted in 1970. In 1973, the United States Supreme Court in Roe v. Wade legalized abortion nationwide, and in 1983, in Bolger v. Young's Drug Products Corp., the Supreme Court struck down as unconstitutional the last remaining Comstock law, which made it a crime to send through the mails unsolicited advertisements for contraceptives.

It is the policy of Planned Parenthood Federation of America to protect the right of each individual to have access to the facts about reproductive health and human sexuality. Planned Parenthood opposes censorship, including efforts to bar information or ban or eliminate materials from educational institutions, libraries, or programs receiving public funds. Planned Parenthood is proud of its history of overcoming attempts to censor information about birth control and sexuality.

We are concerned that the Meese Commission, in the guise of fighting pornography, may signal a revival of "Comstockery," the censorship and suppression that we thought had been left behind in America's development as an informed and caring society.

MAX LILLIENSTEIN

I am Maxwell J. Lillienstein, legal counsel to the American Booksellers Association, a trade association consisting of more than 4000 members and 6000 stores. Our membership accounts for the sale of more than 80 percent of the books of general interest sold by bookstores.

In the last several years, our members have experienced an escalating number of incidents involving formal and informal censorship.

In Florida, a bookseller, who carried a broad line of popular books, specialized in books intended for members of the gay, lesbian, and feminist communities. One-third of the books he carried in stock fell into these categories. By invoking a local zoning ordinance, the authorities compelled him to remove almost all of those books if they contained sexual descriptions or depictions. His alternative was either to commence a costly legal battle or to be closed down as a "public nuisance." He chose the path of least resistance and removed the books, many of which are regularly carried by large retail chain stores.

One year ago a group in Idaho persuaded a local television station that books by a well-known author, V.C. Andrews, fostered incest. The subsequent press and television publicity persuaded other booksellers in the area to withdraw the books from their shelves.

Not long ago a bookseller was arrested in a small town in Alabama pursuant to a local ordinance that made it a crime to sell "obscene materials" to minors. She had sold a copy of <u>Playboy</u> magazine to a 16 year old who, by the prosecutor's own admission, appeared to be more than 18 years of age. But for the fact that she was born and raised in the town and produced her minister as a character witness at the trial, she might have been placed in jail.

Well-reviewed sex education books, intended for teenage audiences, are often stocked in a back room or under the counter after a visit from a well-meaning police officer, citizens group, or minister.

These are several examples of a dangerous and pernicious trend toward censorship of books, magazines, and motion pictures that deal explicitly with the subject of sex.

I am not speaking of the kinds of books and magazines that can only be purchased in "adult" bookstores located in the seedy part of town. I am speaking of popular novels, historical romances, sex education books, and magazines like <u>Playboy</u>. The widespread popularity of books by Jean Auel, Harold Robbins, Jacqueline Suzanne, Judith Krantz, Sidney Sheldon, and hundreds of other authors, suggests that the American reading public does not find offensive books containing frank discussions of sexual conduct. If freedom of expression, guaranteed by the First Amendment, is to have meaning, books and magazines may not be banned or restricted in any way simply because they are offensive to some.

I have asked to testify at the New York hearings of the federal Commission on Pornography on three different occasions, indicating that I, and perhaps some booksellers, could provide the commission with an important perspective. Only on January 10th did I receive a reply, either to my telephone calls or to a letter mailed more than one month ago. The commission has refused the American Booksellers Association an opportunity to testify.

If Congress enacts laws that increase the scope of books, magazines, motion pictures, and plays that may be censored, we can anticipate increased activity on the part of the vigilante groups and governmental authorities. Most of the arguments for new legislation are based upon horror stories given to the commission about the effects of sado-masochistic and hard-core pornographic material. The fact that the commission is spending so much time to listen to such stories is ironic. In almost every case, the kinds of books and photographs and magazines and conduct described by commission witnesses are already in violation of existing statutes. If this commission is objective, as it claims to be, it will make a serious effort to find out what, if anything, can be accomplished by enacting additional legislation.

ANTHONY SCHULTE

I am Anthony Schulte, executive vice president of Random House, and also a member and recent past chairman of the Freedom to Read Committee of the Association of American Publishers. I and many other publishers are extremely concerned with the increasing prevalence of a mentality that favors legislating, at every level -- local, state, and federal -- against the freedom of expression that is essential not only for literature and reading, but for the very essence of the American pluralistic society itself.

I am speaking not only of the climate in which the government would restrict the public's access to information on its workings under the rubric of national security classification; in which a government leaker can be prosecuted and convicted of espionage; in which juries are awarding immense libel verdicts against the media, including book publishers, seemingly for carrying a message offensive to the tastes or values of some part of the public. Rather, I am specifically talking about a climate in which John Gardner's Grendel can be removed from a twelfth grade high school curriculum in the state of California unless all of the parents of all the senior students give their permission for it to be taught; in which Judy Blume's widely praised children's book Deenie can be removed from elementary school libraries in an upper-middle-class suburban county in Georgia because of isolated parental protests; in which J.D. Landis' novel The Sisters Impossible can be withdrawn by the school board from the school library in a town in Oklahoma where one of the town's "leading citizens" objected to the words "hell" and "fart" and its promulgation of "negative values." I'm speaking of the climate in which a prominent and respected New York book publisher had to withdraw from distribution a seriously intended sex education photographic-and-text book for children and parents called Show Me, which had been declared not obscene in several court tests; in which some school publishers have found it necessary to publish expurgated versions of Romeo and Juliet for classroom teaching purposes; and in which even Huckleberry Finn could be removed from the curriculum at certain schools in Virginia as being offensive or racist.

In this climate, a broad range of non-obscene books for adults and for teenagers can be attacked with the support of segments of the community under so-called minors access and display laws. Though such laws have repeatedly been held to be unconstitutional in such states as Colorado, Georgia, and most recently Virginia, they keep coming back in other states, always re-fashioned. They always encourage local authorities or private individuals to put formal or informal pressure on book stores to remove or to withhold from display and sale the works of writers ranging from Judy Blume to John Updike, and from Jean Auel to John Steinbeck. In an Orwellian example of the impact of these statutes, the leading department store in Atlanta actually stopped ordering all new titles from all publishers for a period of several months until the Georgia statute was tested, and of course found wanting, in court. Even Atlanta's best-established purveyor of books, could not run the risk of deciding which titles might run afoul of this law.

Who is to decide which shall be considered obscene or pornographic or beyond the protection of the First Amendment: the government -- local, state, or federal -- a commission, or the market place in which authors, publishers, book reviewers, and readers come together?

In 1970, another federally appointed commission on obscenity and pornography proposed a model statute that the Association of American Publishers and its Freedom to Read Committee considered very carefully and found acceptable. It would place no restrictions, state or federal, on the sale of sexually explicit material that consenting adults choose to read. As publishers, we had no difficulty accepting the proposition that there should be some limitation on the sale or availability of sexually explicit materials to minors so long as these restrictions did not interfere with the rights of adult buyers and readers. We accepted further the notion that unwilling passers-by, as well as minors, should not have displays or promotion for such material thrust upon them in an unavoidable fashion.

These principles seem just as valid for today's America as they did 15 years ago.

ARLENE CARMEN

I grew up during the McCarthy era and became a charter member of The Silent Generation. I have never forgotten the fear that drove my parents to close the windows and turn down the volume as we listened to Paul Robeson sing "A Ballad for Americans." It was one of the minor chilling effects of that investigation into "Godless" Communism.

Thirty years later, the Meese Commission is following this tarnished and discredited example of democracy in action. The timing and tone of the hearings only masks their real agenda. Pornography is a red herring, a scapegoat. The clear and resounding subtext of these hearings is that all sex -- save monogamous, heterosexual, married sex -- is bad.

Now, I know a little bit about scapegoating from years of work with prostitutes on the streets of this city. We can get away with treating them as we do because we have dehumanized, depersonalized, and stereotyped them. It's the way we make any despised group inconsequential, and their humanity invisible. We can then blame them for all of our social ills. The Meese Commission is easily recognized as an offspring of the Moral Majority, which in an unholy alliance has adopted the rhetoric of antipornography feminists. Frightened that America's drift toward permissiveness and promiscuity in recent years will destroy us, they are seeking to tighten the laws that threaten our valued traditions. These "traditions," are centered around the sexual activities of women, like birth control, abortion, and sex outside of marriage, but they include as well the sexual freedom of lesbian and gay people. The solution of these protectors of our values is to make laws that curtail, if not forbid, our changing sexual mores. Religion has historically been a major force in the control of sex and anything that threatens that control is interpreted as dangerous to society.

We are being asked to ignore the commission's lopsided choice of witnesses, suspend our critical faculties, and believe that domestic violence and rape will be eliminated by the suppression of nude photographs; that birth control information and abortion services will become unnecessary in a society that recognizes, as Father Bruce Ritter recently said, that pornography is ". . . a major attack on the core institution of our nation -- the family"; and that gays and lesbians may be denied their civil rights because their sexuality is encouraged by pornographic images.

The Meese Commission gives every indication that it not only proposes to curtail our First Amendment rights, but to control the way each of us live out our lives. The freedom of the individual and rights of conscience will have no place in a society where government espouses a particular religious view of morality, one that has no room for deviation from the norm.

The road to thought and behavior control is short, narrow, and dangerous. Hopefully we will be able to set up roadblocks that will prevent the commission from leading us back to those dark and painful days of the McCarthy era.

BETTY FRIEDAN

I want to express my view, on behalf of a great many
women in this country, feminists and believers in human
rights, that this current move to introduce censorship in the
United States in the guise of suppressing pornography is
extremely dangerous to women. It is extremely dangerous to
the rights of women as well as men to speak and think freely
and to fight for our basic rights, to control our lives, our
bodies, and have some degree of economic and political
equality.

There is a dangerous attempt to use a feminist smoke
screen and even to claim that this antipornography
suppression legislation is a weapon against sex
discrimination and a weapon to liberate women from the
degradation of pornography. Now, I speak as someone who has
no particular liking for pornography and I must say that I
don't indulge in it much. I find a lot of it -- I haven't
seen so much of it -- very boring, and I don't find it
particularly titillating, but I recognize the right of others
who choose to be titillated in that way. And I do find
terribly dangerous the move to suppress sexually explicit
material in books or television. My own book, The Feminine
Mystique, which had something to do with putting a name to
the problems oppressing women, 28 years ago, and helped to
start the modern women's movement, was suppressed as
pornographic. Why, I don't know. Its only passion was for
the personhood of women. It was suppressed as pornographic

in libraries in the Midwest, as I believe Mr. Vonnegut's book was, and certain books by Mark Twain and others. I even think _Alice in Wonderland_ was suppressed by this particular library.

If the antipornography legislation, the suppression of pornography, was passed, the first targets of it would be feminist books, would be books like _Our Bodies, Ourselves_, would be books giving women control of their own bodies. The forces that are behind the antipornography legislation, are those that would take away the right of a woman to decide when and whether and how many times to bear a child, to control her own body. They are the very forces that would even suppress books that show women in roles other than sex objects, show women in nontraditional roles, as astronauts or vice-presidents or doctors, lawyers. We have to ask, what are they up to in this sideshow, this circus about suppressing pornography?

You know, some pornography certainly does degrade women. It also degrades men and it degrades sex. The pornography that pushes violence is particularly deplorable. But the forces that want to suppress pornography are not in favor of suppressing guns. They are not in favor of legislation -- they would undo legislation -- protecting women and children from actual violence. What are they up to?

The ultimate obscenity in America is murderous violence, is the attempt to get rid of our liberties and our freedoms that have made democracy the shining light of the world. And the ultimate obscenity is also poverty, and those who profit from the poverty of others.

Underneath the sideshow, they are trying to excite the passions of the people against ideas -- sexually titillating or repulsive sexually -- but ideas, not actual deeds, not violence, not the obscenity of poverty -- to take our attention away while we are being manipulated in this country, being manipulated, and our rights are being threatened. I call the obscenity that threatens us the obscenity of taking away school lunch from children and milk supplements from babies and some of the medical benefits from old people and reducing Social Security. This is the obscenity. For women there is a particular danger -- the feminization of poverty -- and I deplore that even a very few feminists have been diverted by the issues of pornography from the basic protection of all our rights. Now, I urge all women to have their eyes opened to the dangers to our basic rights by the pushing of antipornography legislation.

TEN WAYS TO COMBAT CENSORSHIP

- Speak out to inform people:

  - about the commission's bias;
  - that the social sciences are far from a consensus about a causal link between pornography and criminal behavior;*
  - about the commission's flagrant disregard for the dangers of censorship;

- Share Meese Commission Exposed with friends, colleagues, press, public policy makers and organizations, including literary, artistic, religious, social, and legal groups;

- Inform public officials -- federal, state and local -- about the dangers of censorship to a free and diversified society;

- Express your views to the larger community through newspaper letter-to-the editor columns;

- Seek public forums through organizations to which you belong for expressing concerns about censorship;

- If your local retail stores are under attack for carrying the "wrong" ideas, initiate a petition for freedom of expression among friends, neighbors, church, civic and school groups. The principle at stake is not offensiveness, but the freedom to choose what to read;

- Speak out against new obscenity laws and prosecutions;

- Enlist others in the fight against censorship. Talk to friends, neighbors and colleagues. To persuade effectively, start with specific needs and interests of your listeners;

  Many people who regard themselves as First Amendment supporters hate whatever it is they call "porn." Explain how measures to remove pornography are an opening wedge to repression (and no more effective in stopping sexually-explicit expression in this day of the Xerox machine and VCR than Prohibition was in stopping bootlegging and bathtub gin.)

- Be prepared to separate myth from reality when political candidates pander to fears;

- Support NCAC's work to defend the right to read by becoming an NCAC Friend. (See page **46.**)

---

* For an excellent overview, see Making Sense of Research on Pornography, a monograph by Thelma McCormack, professor of sociology at York University. Dr. McCormack is president of the Canadian Sociology and Anthropology Association. Reprints are available from NCAC.

To support the work of the National Coalition Against Censorship and the right to read, one can become an NCAC Friend. To become a "Friend," send your name, address and zip with a tax-deductible contribution of $25 or more to National Coalition Against Censorship, 132 West 43 Street, New York, New York 10036. "Friends" receive NCAC's quarterly newsletter, Censorship News and publications such as Books on Trial, a report of the organization's special program on countering censorship in the schools.

 *I WANT TO DEFEND THE RIGHT TO READ*
TO SEE
TO LEARN
TO KNOW
*and be a Friend of the **National Coalition Against Censorship**.*

Here's my contribution of ☐ *$25* ☐*$35* ☐ *$50* ☐ *$100 Other: $*_____
(Friends receive Censorship News, reports, other information.)

*NAME*_____

*ADDRESS*_____

*CITY*_____*STATE*_____*ZIP*_____

Please make your tax-deductible check payable to the National Coalition Against Censorship Inc. and mail it to us at 132 West 43rd Street, New York, N.Y. 10036.